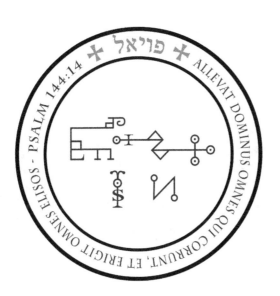

The Institute for Hermetic Studies
Monograph Series # 7

Wisdom's Bliss
and
Khamael's Spear

∞

Mark Stavish, M.A.
IHS Founder & Director of Studies

with

Alfred DeStefano III
Series Editor

Wisdom's Bliss & Khamael's Spear

The Institute for Hermetic Studies
Monograph Series # 7

Copyright © 2016 Mark Stavish

Email: info@hermeticinstitute.org
Website: www.hermeticinstitute.org

The sigil of Poiel at the front of this book was created by

∼ Fr. John Kadai ∼

INSTITUTE FOR HERMETIC STUDIES

MONOGRAPH SERIES

The Institute for Hermetic Studies provides high quality, in-depth monographs for both the academic and practical study of Western esotericism. Designed to be of value to both the professional researcher and practicing student, IHS Monographs contain detailed references, annotations, and listings of source material for further research by the reader. Monographs which were originally issued in PDF as Special Reports by the Institute for Hermetic Studies have been revised and updated.

TITLES IN THE SERIES

Introduction to Hermeticism – Its Theory and Practice
The Theory & Practice of Enochian Magic
Drawing Down the Life of Heaven – Magic in the Renaissance
How to Develop Your Psychic Abilities
Mercury's Children – Shamanic & Hermetic Practices
Studies in Poltergeists, Obsession, & Possession

Acknowledgments

Thank you to **Marc DiCaprio**, **Wade Lane**, **Laurie Miller**, and **Brian Osborne** for their continuous financial support of the Institute for Hermetic Studies and its publishing projects.

In addition, we wish to make a special acknowledgement of the tireless support Kathryn Webb-DeStefano has provided to Alfred as Editor of the Institute for Hermetic Studies Series. This is also true of my wife, Andrea Nerozzi, and children, Luke and Nathaniel, as they have collectively been the rock upon which the Institute for Hermetic Studies has been built.

Introduction

Wisdom's Bliss and *Khamael's Spear* were the first Special Reports produced for the Institute for Hermetic Studies. The idea of creating specialized papers addressing a single topic in-depth came out of a luncheon conversation with Susan Lafetteri at the Amber Indian Restaurant in Moosic, Pennsylvania. Susan, previously of Pawtucket, Rhode Island, had moved to Northeastern Pennsylvania at the same time Andrea (my wife-to-be) and I were moving to Providence. We briefly met after a presentation on Qabala I gave at the local Unity Church in Wilkes-Barre. About ten years would pass before we would meet again. By then I was getting published and she was starting a new career as a publishing consultant. She suggested the idea of "Special Reports" to grab readers' attention—and it worked. In many ways, the current Institute for Hermetic Studies Monograph Series is a direct result of that conversation over lentils and basmati rice on a sunny day in October 2004. Marc Thorner, of Thorner Graphics, generously produced our original covers using a unique Egyptian design.

The point is simple: you never know the effect someone will have on the course of your life, so be as generous as you can (without being foolish).

That is really the basis of these two papers and their lessons. For too long, students of Western esotericism—and of ceremonial magic in particular—have crucified themselves on the Pillar of Severity, resulting in placing a great deal of emphasis on their "mercurial" properties of mind. Mercury, however, is dual. It can help us to reconcile opposites and bring people and ideas together, or it can tear them apart. Unfortunately, as a result, Western occultists have as a group been overly critical, manifesting in self-destructive thoughts, words, and actions. The counterbalance to this is, of course, Mercy, or a greater sense of generosity and interdependence with others. Since we are talking about esotericism, these "others" are both visible and invisible, both known and unknown to us. By cultivating mercy or kindness, we open ourselves up to a host of relationships and opportunities. It is no matter that this is the name given to the spiritual domain ruled by Jupiter, the most desirable planet in astrology for those who seek health, happiness, and wealth.

At the same time, this sense of Mercy must be balanced out by a realization of our need for personal strength and (to a certain degree) boundaries, so that we are not taken advantage of, nor do we allow ourselves to be weakened or even destroyed by others. When *Khamael's Spear* was written, it was done so in response to the growing flames of terrorism and war present at the time. It was hoped that readers would be able to use the methods presented in a very real transformative sense, to transform their own anger and frustration as well as the general energies of their communities and those who wished harm on others. In no way was this meant to be some kind of "instant" transformation wherein the world would be turned into a Utopia. No: we simply want to take the edge off of the energies of destruction present, for individuals, nations, and the world as a whole. Sometimes that is all you can do, and that is all that is needed.

Students of modern magical and initiatic orders will notice that these two essays address the energies of the spheres on the Tree of Life known as Chesed and Geburah, ruled by Jupiter and Mars respectively. Both of these essays and their attendant practices will assist practitioners in getting a deeper understanding of the energies of these spheres, as well as open students to the possibility of genuine initiation in them, thereby bringing about a transformation of personal consciousness.

I wish each of you the best in your journey on the Path of Return.

Sincerely,

Mark Stavish

Director of Studies
Institute for Hermetic Studies
19 September 2016

Part I

Wisdom's Bliss

~

Developing Compassion

in

Western Esotericism

If you want to advance on the esoteric path...you should make an effort to Serve. The first principle to be applied on the Path, in relation to our world, is that we should not seek to get more through the esoteric Path but to become more.

— Jean Dubuis

Monograph Overview

- The Tree of Life in Traditional Western Esotericism
- The Adept's Oath and Its Meaning
- The Tree of Life: A View from Chesed

Introduction

The Qabalistic Tree of Life, or *Otz Chaiim*, has been one of the principal symbols of Western esotericism for nearly a thousand years. Adopted by Christian and Hermetic mystics in the fourteenth century, it quickly grew beyond its early Jewish roots into the core symbol for a vast array of alchemical, magical, mystical, astrological, and general esoteric work over the next six hundred years.

Since its early origins in the ninth or tenth century, the Tree has seen many variations, including some exceptionally modern ones that modify the basic design for specific alchemical, astrological, or meditative practices.[1] However, despite these modifications, the fundamental design and function of the Tree of Life has remained the same. As one modern authority stated it, "Thus do we see in the Tree [of Life] a glyph of the soul of man and the universe, and in the legends associated with it the history of the evolution of the soul and the Way of Initiation."[2]

While it is not necessary to enter into a detailed discussion of the nature of the Tree and how it reflects the interactions of microcosm and macrocosm, it is important to point out that the Tree reflects several foundational esoteric principles. The most essential of these principles relate to the densification of energy into matter and the interdependence of matter, energy, and consciousness as they relate to the origin of Being. This reflects an evolution which may be sped up through the initiatic process; when authentic, this process imitates the path of nature with increased efficiency. We hesitate to use the word "authentic," but it is important to note that there are Paths that work and those that don't. There are also paths which lead consciousness back to the One, and those that simply free it from material bondage to wander in the astral realms.

> Originally, man was potentially an eternal being. The nature of the Absolute is such that man cannot

---

[1] See: Frater Albertus, *The Seven Rays of the Q.B.L.* (Salt Lake City, UT: Paracelsus Research Society, 1968); Mark Stavish, "The Portæ Lucis Method of Jean Dubuis" (available online); Gareth Knight, *Experience of the Inner Worlds* (Toddington [UK]: Helios Book Service, 1975).

[2] Dion Fortune, *The Mystical Qabalah* (York Beach, ME: Samuel Weiser, Inc., 2000) 18.

realize himself in the Eternal world. That is to say in the Eternal world, he cannot move from his state of potential being to the state of realized being, or move from Zero to the Infinite.

Through the necessity of his Becoming, man voluntarily "descends" into space- time, into the worlds of progressively denser matter. This is involution. When he has gathered the necessary elements, man starts his way back up: he leaves the denser worlds; this is evolution. The end of the journey, the return, is his reintegration into Eternity. During this journey, both on the descending path and on the ascending path, there are ten stages. Man's consciousness must adapt to the ten levels of energy and matter of Creation.[3]

In addition, the Tree illustrates a triune hierarchy of "Causes": active principles ruling the invisible and visible worlds. The Primary Cause is the most powerful and is closest to the absolute nature of Being, or what the Qabalist calls the "Nothingness." This Primary Cause is mostly concerned with the first and second (and some say third) levels of the Tree. The Secondary Causes[4] are concerned with those parts of the Tree having planetary associations with them—levels three through nine. Their function is the management of the material world from the perspective of the invisible world. Finally, the third Cause is our material

---

[3] Jean Dubuis, *Fundamentals of Esoteric Knowledge* (Wheaton, IL: Triad Publishing, 2000) 6.

[4] See the writings of Johannes Trithemius and Cornelius Agrippa for details on the Secondary Causes.

world, dominated by the First and Second Causes, but with a barrier that allows humanity to have free will and thus to act freely in this material domain. This is, of course, not without associated consequences—good or ill.

It is this "free will"—the freedom to heed the voice of intuition or ignore it—which allows humanity to develop genuine inner freedom based upon earthly experiences.

> In the most general sense, the symbolism of the tree denotes the life of the cosmos: its consistence, growth, proliferation, generative and regenerative process. It stands for inexhaustible life, and is therefore equivalent to a symbol of immortality... The tree, with its roots underground and its branches rising to the sky, symbolizes an upward trend and is therefore related to other symbols, such as the ladder and the mountain, which stand for the general relationship between the "three worlds."[5]

The Tree is also found in alchemy and symbolizes the various stages, elements, and forces in the Great Work. From this we can also see that the Tree can exist on several levels: material, psychic, or spiritual. "The Secrets of John Dee" illustrates a tree for each metal/planet and demonstrates its symbolic use in alchemy during the early "Rosicrucian" period.[6]

---

[5] J. E. Cirlot, *A Dictionary of Symbolism* (New York: Dorset Press, 1991) 346.

[6] Gordon James, *The Secrets of John Dee* (Edmonds, WA: Holmes Publishing Group, 1995).

Freedom and Initiation

The impulse to attain freedom from the harsh effects of material life, to enter into the invisible, and to return to the source of our Being happens both collectively and individually. However, despite the power of groups, all evolution is ultimately an individual choice and accomplished by individual effort. This is not to say groups are not important, as they supply mutual support, encouragement, direction, and instruction; however, the actual work is done by each individual. We may "ride" on the collective strength of an initiatic or esoteric organization (or even culture) to which we belong, but that will only take us to the door of self-mastery. To enter into the "Invisible Fraternity" we must prove our worthiness through the quality of our presence, a presence which reflects the Greek injunction from above the portal of the Temple of Apollo at Delphi in Ancient Greece—*Gnothi Seauton*: "Know Thyself."

This state of "knowing oneself" is also called "Knowledge and Conversation" with one's Holy Guardian Angel or Messenger. This messenger is none other than our Divine spark or flame, that part of us which is most closely connected to the Primary Cause, which allows us to be connected to the rest of creation on a deep, powerful, and meaningful level.

This Knowledge and Conversation is not self-mastery, but the first real step toward it. True self-mastery occurs when there is no sense of separation from Creation while retaining the awareness that we exist as individual sparks of consciousness.[7]

---

[7] The final step is when we merge ourself completely with the Infinite. This requires, in qabalistic language, that we "Cross the Abyss" from

To progress in this "next leg" of a very long journey, it is important that we seek to be of assistance to others in their journey, even if they are not conscious of the fact that they too, simply as a matter of being here with us, are also on a voyage of self-discovery. We can also help those who are discarnate, as well as all animal, mineral, and vegetable life we depend on for our material existence.

In many ways, the more we seek to serve others in their growth, and the less we worry about our own state of internal affairs, the more we benefit from our esoteric practices. Service is the true hallmark of an initiate. Selfless service is the work of the adept. If we seek to be an adept then we must act like one.

In this document we have provided an outline for students, giving several methods whereby they can assist themselves, their fellow spiritual co-workers, and their communities. Some might be tempted to expand this to include the world as a whole, but that is not necessary. By taking care of our own backyards—be it our family, business, or lodge—we strengthen the global community both visibly and invisibly. We also focus the energy, allowing it to have practical and at times visible results. Perhaps more importantly, we follow the Biblical injunction to pay more attention to the "log" in our own eye, than the speck in our neighbor's.

It is not world saviors that we are seeking here, but community ones. *Avatars* come in all sizes and shapes. As esoteric students seeking adepthood and self-mastery, we are *de facto* "avatars in training." To fail to accept this is to ignore the true function of esoteric practice: to

---

Chesed to Binah, and continue onward to Kether. A discussion of this is beyond the scope of the present monograph.

help ourselves first, so that we can more efficiently help others in their Becoming. Students of Qabala and Alchemy are particularly aware of the importance of the avatar[8] or Unknown Superior[9] in traditional Western esotericism, and their intimate relationship with the sphere of Chesed on the Tree of Life.

The great advantage of working with the invisible forces with which we are concerned is that the assistance we seek to render does not rely on material wealth, proximity, or direct contact to be effective.

The Bodhisattva Vow

In the "Bodhisattva Vow" of Buddhism, a subject many students of Western esotericism are familiar with, the student is advised to "take refuge" from suffering in the three vehicles of the Buddha, Dharma, and Guru.[10] In addition, they state that the purpose for performing their meditations is to seek enlightenment not for themselves, but to assist others—just as have the Bodhisattvas before them and to whom they are indebted for the vitality of their tradition and practice.

---

[8] "Avatar" is Sanskrit and is derived from locations on river banks where one can descend into the water. As such, the term is used to refer to a highly awakened being that "descends" from the spiritual domain in order to "enter" into matter and assist humanity in some form.

[9] Also referred to as *Supérieur Inconnu* in French and *Unbekannte Oberin* in German. This also refers to the Illuminati.

[10] The Three Jewels of Buddhism have their reflection in the Sangha (Lodge), Dharma (Teachings of the Tradition), and Guru (Lodge Master, Teacher, and Instructor).

The human ideal of the Mahayana ("great vehicle" Buddhism) is the bodhisattva, the "enlightened being" who practices wisdom and compassion and strives for enlightenment for the welfare of all beings. According to the Mahayana, every human being, and indeed every sentient being, is destined one day to become a fully enlightened Buddha, just like Buddha Shakyamuni. Those who came before and already attained Buddhahood are found, as mentioned, throughout time and space.[11]

Bodhichitta is the inner heartfelt attitude that we possess (and increase through practice) to attain enlightenment to further assist others. It is our inner idealistic notions and utopian fantasies being given a genuine and meaningful task and the means to carry it out.

The Vow of the Adeptus Exemptus

In his description of the work and obligation of an *Adeptus Exemptus*, Aleister Crowley writes the following:[12]

---

[11]Reginald A. Ray, *Indestructible Truth* (New York: Shambhala, 2000) 68.

[12]In the Golden Dawn, students who passed to the Adeptus Exemptus grade undertook a re-examination of the Adeptus Minor ($5° = 6°$) material in order to obtain a deeper understanding and practical knowledge of it. This, in turn, led to a further study of the Neophyte Degree ($0° = 0°$). Additionally, as one progressed through the additional higher degrees, a similar revisiting of the lower, or Elemental Degrees, would take place. The entire process of the higher grades of the Golden Dawn is but a reflection of where the student has come from. This is seen in the *Zelator* Adeptus Minor grade, which re-studies the $0° = 0°$ up until *Adeptus* Adeptus Minor, which studies the $4° = 7°$; the $6° =$

The Grade of Adeptus Exemptus confers authority to govern the two lower Orders of R. C. and G. D.[13]

The Adept must prepare and publish a thesis setting forth his knowledge of the Universe, and his proposals for its welfare and progress. He will thus be known as a leader of a school of thought.

(Éliphas Lévi's *La clef des grand mystères*, the works of Swedenborg, von Eckartshausen, Robert Fludd, Paracelsus, Newton, Bolyai, Loyola, etc., are examples of such successes.)

He will have attained all but the supreme summits of meditation, and should be *already prepared to perceive that the only possible course for him is to devote himself utterly to helping his fellow creatures* [emphasis added].[14]

At this point, the aspirant takes the Vow of the Exempt Adept:

I gave moreover the signs of the grades from $0° = 0\square$ to $7° = 4\square$.[15]

$5\square$ studies the Portal, and so on. The $8° = 3\square$ studies the $6° = 5\square$ and the $9° = 2\square$ studies the $7° = 4\square$. For more information see: Pat Zalewski, *Secret Inner Order Rituals of the Golden Dawn* (Tempe, AZ: Falcon Press, 1988) and Appendix II in Ellic Howe, *The Magicians of the Golden Dawn* (York Beach, ME: Samuel Weiser, Inc., 1978). (Note that according to Pat Zalewski, Appendix II is inaccurately titled, and reflects the work of the *Theoricus* Adeptus Minor.)

[13]Crowley's material reflects a bias of the Golden Dawn and its offshoot traditions regarding this degree.

[14]Aleister Crowley, et al., *Commentaries on the Holy Books and other Papers*, in *The Equinox*, Vol. Four (York Beach, ME: Samuel Weiser, Inc., 1996) 14.

[15]These degree Signs are from the Golden Dawn tradition and can be

Then did I take upon myself the Great Obligation as follows:

1. I, O.M., &c. [the Magical Names assumed by the candidate up to this point], a member of the Body of God, hereby bind myself on behalf of the whole Universe, even as we are now physically bound unto the cross of suffering:
2. that I will lead a pure life, as a devoted servant of the Order:
3. that I will understand all things:
4. that I will love all things:
5. that I will perform all things and endure all things:
6. that I will continue in the Knowledge and Conversation of My Holy Guardian Angel:
7. that I will work without attachment:
8. that I will work in truth:
9. that I will rely only upon myself:
10. that I will interpret every phenomenon as a particular dealing of God with my soul.

And if I fail herein, may my pyramid be profaned, and the Eye be closed upon me!

All this did I swear and seal with a stroke upon the Bell.[16]

---

found in Crowley's *Magick* (San Francisco: Weiser Books, 1997) 616-17. Other schools, such as Martinism or variations of Rosicrucianism, do not use these Signs.

[16] Aleister Crowley, *John St. John: The Paris Working* in *The Equinox*, Vol. I, No. 1 (London: Simpkin, Marshall, Hamilton, Kent & Co., Ltd., 1909) 9-10.

The *Oath of the Adeptus Exemptus* is similar in tone and purpose to the Bodhisattva Vow. The grade of *Adeptus Exemptus* relates to the sphere of Chesed on the Tree of Life, and each of the ten points listed is a sphere for the Tree as perceived from the perspective of Chesed. Each sphere has its own qualities, energetic nature, and set of correspondences with the material and psychic worlds. Each in its own way can also be experienced as its own little world. The nature of these "worlds" relates directly to the qualities of consciousness that are required to awaken (and developed as a result of awakening) that sphere within our psyche.

Chesed is referred to as the *Cohesive or Receptacular Intelligence*; it "contains the Holy Powers" of all the spheres of the Tree of Life. All of the powers of the spheres of the Tree of Life are in some manner affected by Divine Mercy. Through it, the highest spiritual powers manifest into reality and contain within themselves the fundamental seed of unity, expansion, and happiness.

On a cosmological level we can get some ideas of Chesed that will help us better understand its more personal psychic (as well as mundane) aspects.

Notes on Chesed

Chesed is the preserving, all-loving father figure, who continually builds up, organizes, and preserves what has been created. It is the "First Day of Creation,"[17] or the formulation of a concrete idea out of the abstract. The

---

[17] The remaining "Days of Creation" follow *Mezla* on the Tree of Life, ending with Malkuth as "Shabbati" (Saturn), the Day of Rest.

opposite of Chesed (the "building up" facility) is Geburah, the destructive facility. We consider Geburah "destructive" only insofar as it destroys what is outdated, ineffectual, and no longer needed. It performs the act of sacrifice—to make sacred.

Chesed is concerned with *causes* and *long-term effects*. It is global in scope. In distinction to this broad-reaching scheme is the person whose view is only concerned with details, who always appears to be a victim of chance: the citizen of Malkuth.

We cannot be too firm on this point. To function in or under the influence of Chesed, in some way, is to take the abstract, make it concrete, and move it into an area of practical functioning on the psychic and material levels. It is for this reason that we see so much emphasis on this being the sphere of the "Unknown Superiors" or "Invisible Masters" of esotericism. Being possessed of this gigantic perspective, they are able to formulate methods and schools of teaching that are in accordance with the age in which they exert their influence.

Practical Qabala is quite clear about this: if we seek to understand and experience the influence of these "superbeings," we must resonate near their level. To do this, we must raise our level of consciousness (i.e., our thinking and feeling) beyond day-to-day concerns (Malkuth) or internal images and subconscious distractions (Yesod). Focused and purposeful construction and use of images as meditative and ritualistic tools (Hod) can be bent toward this end. At this point, we can begin to experience some of the influences of the broad, compassionate, evolutionary, and creative force we are calling Chesed.

It is important to note that all of this powerful influence is mediated through the focal point of Self, or Tiphareth on the Tree of Life. If our idea of Self is broad, embracing, and tolerant, then the greater will be our ability to take into ourselves the expansive influences of Chesed. If, however, we have not adequately purged ourselves of pettiness and narrowness, our ability to make use of the influences of Chesed will be comparatively limited. Thus, the Illuminated Adept, the politician, and the industrialist all clearly fall under the influences of this sphere.

The world needs—and will always need—leaders of varying scopes in its different fields and areas of activity. True leaders are able to see the "causes and effects" (the Path from Chesed to Netzach): "the big picture." The forces and influences of Chesed are continually expressed; each of us responds to them in our own way. However, when understood correctly, it becomes increasingly clear what Jesus meant when he said that we cannot hide our light under a bushel.[18]

If we consciously contact the energies of Chesed, we will then be consciously changed. If we accept the role of "leader," then others will look to us for assistance and direction. If we try to deny this new role—this *responsibility*—we will find ourselves stunted in our future evolution.

The four "fours" of the tarot (in Pentacles, Cups, Swords, and Wands) represent the four qualities that manifest in the personality who has experienced Chesed, to their own degree and in accordance with their new-found purpose or mission.

---

[18] Matthew 5:15.

Perfected Work – Wands
Lord of Pleasure – Cups
Rest from Strife – Swords
Earthly Power – Pentacles

These cards and titles represent how the energies of Chesed have a practical and meaningful effect on our consciousness and life through all of the "Elements" of which consciousness and life as we know it is composed.

Perfected Work. Air – intellect; ideas.

Lord of Pleasure. Water – emotions; the psychic realm.

Rest from Strife. Fire – energy; no resistance to will.

Earthly Power. Earth – material mastery, as our ideas are clear and focused, our energy irresistible, and our emotions and psychic creations are expansive, joyful, and unaffected by external circumstances in a world of change.

Four corresponds to balance (i.e., stability of the quaternary) as well as a self-perfecting state. Balance is "imperturbability," or the ability to remain calm and focused in any situation. This "centered" state, where our energies flow from within rather than as reactions to what is going on outside of us, is the basis for self-mastery. Only in a calm yet dynamic state, ready for action, can we say that we have integrated the experiences of Tiphareth (Knowledge and Conversation with our Inner Master or Holy Guardian Angel) and Geburah (purification and integration of the residual chaotic forces in the personality) that leads to an ever-present state of openness, energy, compassion, and wisdom.

In many ways, the expression of power over the Elements as expressed in the physical world of Malkuth—as well as within our personality—when under the influence of Chesed is like taking the experience of Tiphareth and multiplying it by 100.[19]

When seen in this light, the archetypal influences that create an "ideal adept" become more practical and attainable. In addition, the Paths leading towards Chesed—the 19th, 20th, and 21st—represent the various ways a highly evolved personality interacts with creation and those around them.

21st **Path.** Gives an expansion of mercy and wisdom, along with mastery of the Laws of Karma (cause and effect) in the psychic and material worlds. This is accompanied by a distinct increase in energy in each of the principle psychic centers, symbolized by the influence of Jupiter (Expansion) on Netzach/Venus—the Seven Secondary Causes, which in each human being are their principal psychic centers.[20] Much of this feeling is directed towards a profound love for humanity and material creation (as expressed by Venus).

---

[19]This may or may not be an arbitrary figure if we consider that there is a Tree, or ten sephiroth, in each Sephirah. In alchemy, it is said that in Tiphareth we make the Philosopher's Stone, but it still must be "Multiplied" two more times, i.e., pushed up two more sephirothic levels to Chesed. In any case, the level of increase is geometric and not arithmetical.

[20]We realize that the number of psychic centers is arbitrary and that some systems use Elemental correspondences rather than planetary ones.

20th **Path.** This is ultimate individuality united to the cosmos: expansion of the power of compassion and mercy in the personality of the adept. This is accompanied by a distinct and profound influx of a refined and elevating energy into the heart, encompassing the visible and invisible worlds. In addition, there is also a distinct practicality to the insights gained, along with clear knowledge of the work that needs to be done under the influence of this experience. This is a result of the influence of Chesed on Virgo as the medium of affecting the Self (Tiphareth).

19th **Path.** This Path is a strengthening of the inner self through purification of the residuals of the material life through a balancing of justice with mercy within one's personal sense of Self.

These experiences can come about either as a direct working of the Paths on the Tree of Life or indirectly through extended work and meditation on the qualities of Jupiter and Chesed in one's evolution. Either way, they will be experienced and integrated if the ideal of the *Adeptus Exemptus*, Awakened Mind, is adhered to.

1. We have already undertaken commitment to the spiritual path and the specifics of a particular tradition or method. This method is demonstrated to be effective through its history (archetypal and/or historical founder who is enlightened), its teachings, and its current expression in the form of a living exponent.

2. We place others before ourselves in a manner that is

positive, empowering, and role-modeling, rather than pathological, co-dependent, and destructive.

3. We consciously attach ourselves to this very high ideal and reinforce it through daily practice.

4. We seek neither to accumulate "merit" nor "karma" for ourselves, nor to alleviate it, but hope that our efforts will assist others in their Becoming. We share any blessings or benefits that might be derived from our practice wholly and freely with others. We "give it away" at the end of each session so as to not "accumulate" it; in being unconcerned with our personal liberation, we transcend duality.

5. We cultivate loving-kindness, joy, compassion, and equanimity towards all beings.

However, fine and noble aspirations are not enough. As one modern authority states:

> The necessity for specialized culture of the will in occult work is a matter upon which most of us are in agreement. In all world progress it is the great driving force. But the will to tread the path is of a higher nature. It is in reality the inner spiritual self acting steadily and unceasingly through the personality. And when, through study and meditation and one-pointed determination to achieve master hood [i.e., the path of the Bodhisattva] this inner self or spiritual will is gradually released and begins to act powerfully in the personality, only then do the real

problems of the path emerge and call for the greatest strength to deal with them.[21]

Summary of the Work to Follow

1. Build the Tree of Life within yourself, while imaging it being constructed above you in the sky. Then, project this image to see a giant Tree of Life in the center of your city.

2. Same as above, but assume the godform of Thoth-Tahuti—the Egyptian god of wisdom and magic, and "dharma guardian" of the Western Esoteric (or Hermetic) Traditions.[22]

3. Same as above, but after assuming the godform, undertake the practice of *tonglen*, to reduce the level of pain and suffering in the world.

4. **The Rite of the Order of Melchizedek.** Gifts, offerings, and Holy Communion with all whom we encounter in our life.

---

[21]Raymund Andrea, FRC, *The Technique of the Master* (San Jose, CA: Rosicrucian Order [AMORC], 1932) 117-18.

[22]Other suitable forms include: Christian Rosenkreutz, the Angel of the Annunciation from "The Alchemical Wedding of Christian Rosenkreutz," Christ, and the Egyptian Goddess Maat.

Basic Practice

The Flashing Sword[23] represents the original descent of Divine energy, or *Mezla*, during the act of creation. Once this act was accomplished, the energy began to rise back again, toward its original source, and this became known to qabalists as "The Rising Serpent." Together, the ascent and descent form a symbolic glyph of the entire creative process that is well known to students of Hermeticism.

When this process of creation is imagined as part of ourselves, we take on the role of creator and created. The Lightning Flash of creation goes through us, and we become re-created on a subtle and interior level. When this energy returns to its source, we are lifted ever so slightly higher on the Path of Return. Our psychic centers, corresponding to the spheres on the Tree, are awakened and brought into harmony with each other, and we become the Adam Kadmon (or Original Being-Man) before the so-called "Fall." In short, since we are in our daily life already "Fallen," by performing this and other esoteric exercises, we take on the role of redeemer of ourselves and creation, or that of Christ. In light of what we have said about the role of the Adept (in particular the Vow of the Adeptus Exemptus), this statement takes on a profound meaning. We no longer look to another to "save" or "enlighten" us, but instead find the ability and responsibility to do so within ourselves. More importantly, we share this with others on a profoundly psychic level.

Always remember to prepare yourself and your area for meditation—using a banishing ritual, attitude of mind, or

---

[23]Much of the material for this section derives from Mark Stavish, "The Flashing Sword" (available online at hermeticinstitute.org).

other means deemed suitable—and to offer a suitable prayer that your work might be fruitful and of benefit to yourself, fellow students on the Path, and humanity in general.

The Flashing Sword

The Technique of "The Flashing Sword" is among one of the most common methods known to Qabalists, yet is one of the least commented upon. Like many esoteric practices, it lends itself to a great deal of sophistication, and can be introduced to beginning students as a practical mnemonic device for learning the basics of the Tree of Life, up to a method for releasing the "Secret Fire" or *Æsch Mezareph*[24] in each of us.

Part One

Visualize a sphere of light above your head. Make it so intense that its center point appears black. Concentrate on this sphere for several minutes. Watch it pulse and grow brighter, hotter, and more intense with each breath. Imagine a ray of light coming down from it piercing the top of your head, or crown area, where the skull bones come together. Feel the ray enter into the center of your head, filling it with brilliant, intense light. Feel a ray of this light move over to the left temple, filling the entire left side of your skull, brain, and face with light. After a minute or two, imagine the ray of light moving over to the right temple, filling it

---

[24] This is an alchemical term and title of an alchemical text, *Purifying Fire*; it also refers to the power of liberation, commonly called *kundalini*.

with light. Meditate on this for a minute or two. Pause now, and visualize these three brilliant spheres of light—the crown, left temple, and right temple—connected by three rays of light from their center points, forming a triangle with a brilliant point of light in its center. Let the brilliance grow, fusing the images into a single sphere of brilliant light.

Let a ray now pass down from the right side to your left shoulder.[25] After a minute or so, let the ray of light continue towards your right shoulder; then to your heart area, below the sternum, and after a minute or so, to your left hip. The ray continues across to your right hip, and then to your pubic bone. After a minute or two of meditation, it continues to the center of your feet (as if you were standing *in* a brilliant ball of light). You can also imagine the energy continuing to the fiery center of the earth.

Each sphere should be brilliant, bright, warm, and vibrant. The lines connecting them should be a brilliant bluish-white color, with sharp, clear edges.

You may end your meditation at this point. If you feel the energy is too intense, or experience a sense of drowsiness or heaviness, withdraw the point of light from your feet and reverse the light, taking the spheres with you, back to Kether, and to the starting point above your head. Let that light then fade to black.

After you acquire competency in this technique, add the Queen's Color Scale to each sphere and vibrate the names for each sphere, in order of highest to lowest (Divine Name – Archangelic – Angelic – Mundane) for each sphere.[26] Meditate on absorbing the energy of the sphere for a minute

---

[25] At each stage, allow a sphere of brilliant light to be formed.
[26] See the accompanying table.

or two, and then move on to the next sphere.

Sephirah	Color	Divine Name	Archangel	Angel	Mundane
Kether	White	Eheieh	Metatron	—	—
Chokmah	Grey	YH	Ratziel	—	—
Binah	Black	YHVH Elohim	Tzaphqiel	Cassiel	Shabbathai
Chesed	Blue	El	Tzadqiel	Sachiel	Tzedek
Geburah	Red	Elohim Gibor	Khamael	Zamael	Madim
Tiphareth	Gold	YHVH Eloah v'Daäth	Raphael	Michael	Shemesh
Netzach	Green	YHVH Tzabaoth	Haniel	Hanael	Nogah
Hod	Orange	Elohim Tzabaoth	Michael	Raphael	Kokab
Yesod	Violet	Shaddai El Chai	Gabriel	Gabriel	Levanah
Malkuth	Mixed[a]	Adonai ha-Aretz	Sandalphon	—	Olam Yesodot

CORRESPONDENCES FOR THE FLASHING SWORD EXERCISE

[a] Equal parts of citrine, olive, russet, and black.

Now repeat the process, this time visualizing the Tree above and around you, finally entering "Malkuth" where you are, or if in a temple, into the altar.

Once this image is completed, perform it for a third time, or simply visualize the Tree if need be, existing in giant proportions, and the energies entering into the center of your town, city, or local focal point if in a dispersed community. Remember to add the side and middle pillars.

Sense the energies entering into yourself, your temple, and your community for the benefit of all beings.

It is critical that you simply open yourself up to these energies and not direct any specific outcome. Simply hold the thought that the energies of Original Creation are being rebalanced in you, your sacred space, and your community.

Part Two

After you have successfully built up the Tree of Life, you may perform Rising on the Planes, or you simply sense yourself in the golden brilliance of Tiphareth, in the close presence of your Inner Self, as if it were whispering in your ear. Assume the god form of Thoth, the Egyptian God of Wisdom and Magic, the Guardian Deity of the Western Esoteric (Hermetic) Traditions.[27]

We strongly urge the use of this god form because of its trans-sectarian nature and association with all of the major (and most minor) Western esoteric traditions in some form. Thus, by using Thoth, we go right to the heart of Western esotericism and avoid the divisive sectarianism of more specialized figures.

> The designation "sons of Hermes"[28] takes us back to the...idea, with the warning that here "Hermes" should not be considered an actual historical personage, but the special spiritual influence that defined the initiatic chain...[29]

As one modern authority states:

> Above all the invocations, there is one that is fundamental—the Formula of the Enterer. This is the

---

[27] For more information on Assumption of the Godform, see: "Notes on the Assumption of the Godform" by Mark Stavish. Available online at hermeticinstitute.org.

[28] Alchemists have often been referred to as "sons of Hermes," as they partake in the ancient mysteries of Khem, or Egypt.

[29] Julius Evola, *The Hermetic Tradition* (Rochester, VT: Inner Traditions, 1995) 210.

invocation of Thoth where the adept forges a magical link between his or herself and the godform. Thoth is the link to our spirit consciousness and the adept must assume his form at the start of any [advanced] rituals, as dictated in the Exordium.[30]

By drawing upon the power of Thoth we can draw from a type of spiritual gene pool of everything that Thoth represents, that in turn gives us the power to command any entity invoked through him. Thoth gives us order in chaos, and he has the power of "accumulation" (for Thoth has recorded everything since the dawning of time) and it is that which we draw upon in our ritual. In psychological terms, Thoth becomes the archetypal doorway to Jung's concept of the "Collective Unconscious." Within the Golden Dawn his power is almost unlimited and transcends that of Osiris.[31]

Part Three

The role of wisdom is only seen in action. Thoth is active in all areas of Egyptian life; Hermes is active instructing in the confecting of the Philosopher's Stone; Mercury is so active that it is volatile, continually relaying messages between the gods, and between the gods and men. Action for the adept is in sacrifice and service to others. The greatest service we can render is to alleviate the suffering of others so that they might be able to have enough mental clarity,

---

[30] See Appendix to Part One of the present text.
[31] Pat Zalewski, *Talismans & Evocations of the Golden Dawn* (Loughborough, Leicestershire: Thoth Publications, 2002) 198.

if only for a moment, to begin the journey of the Path of Return. In doing so, we lift their burden for a moment so that they can "redistribute the load" and carry on more productively when it is placed back on their shoulders.

In Tibetan Buddhism the practice of *tonglen* is considered one of the most important acts an individual can undertake for their personal development: it takes a person out of themselves, and focuses on the needs of others. This practice is not unique to Buddhism; it can be seen in several prayers of the Roman Catholic Church, and in exoteric and esoteric liturgies and rituals. We have given two versions of it here, although many versions of this practice exist. One method utilizes the *Assumption of the Godform*; the second technique does not.

Tonglen ("sending and taking" or "giving and receiving") is the most challenging and powerful of all *Mahayana* practices, but is also undertaken in the *Vajrayana* tradition. *Vajra*, or diamond, refers to the single-pointed indestructible consciousness of the practitioner (as diamonds are the hardest substance known in nature).

Tonglen has some very similar qualities to the lessons of the 31st, 24th, and 11th paths on the Tree of Life.

> Disciples of the mystic way know the meaning of the word suffering and do not turn from it as a depressing theme. They know that it is intimately bound up with the mystical life: for it is precisely those on the way who are called upon to suffer; and if it is not their own suffering, then through their own developing sensitivity they are sympathetically drawn to share in that of others. That is the penalty, far rather the

privilege, of entering upon the way. There is no way of avoiding it. As certainly as the disciple proceeds along the way, will he enter into the suffering of human life. But what is there in this life of more value than trying "to lift a little of the heavy Karma of the world?" There is no greater reward than the heart-spoken gratitude of those whose suffering we have made our own through passing through the shadow in soul with them. Do not retreat from it, but let the scars of human sorrow remain in the soul as a lasting memorial of your compassion and kindness. It is the one thing the Master waits to read there. It is the universal language of Masters and disciples, the mystic bond which unites them into one compassionate fraternity. For what is the ground of the solicitude of the Master, the watchful care which he exercises in training his pupil to share in his own work? Not assuredly to satisfy any personal motives of the disciple, and least of all to meet a personal desire for special powers to demonstrate his ascendancy over his fellow men. It is for one reason only: to share the burden of the Karma of the world. That is the purpose of the way.[32]

31st **Path.** Shin; purification; to raise up and expand consciousness.

24th **Path.** Ayin; used to realize that all experience and things can assist us in our enlightenment.

---

[32]Raymund Andrea, FRC, *The Mystic Path* (San Jose, CA: Rosicrucian Order [AMORC], 1937) 113-14.

11th Path. Air–Mercury; to experience that "Good and Evil" are non-existent on a cosmic level.

The 31st and 24th Paths are a representation of the alchemical Path of Urbigerus and Flamel; they represent a very powerful, dynamic, and straightforward path to Illumination.

Do not be concerned, though, about any harm coming to you from this practice. It is in fact not "you" that is taking on the suffering of others, nor "you" that is transforming it into joy, serenity, or other positive and life-affirming emotions: it is your Inner Self that does the Work. It can also be stated that we do not really affect others as much as we affect our relationships toward them.

> The one thing that you should know for certain is that the only thing that Tonglen could harm is the one thing that has been harming you the most: your own ego, your self-grasping, self-cherishing mind, which is the root of suffering. For if you practice Tonglen as often as possible, this self-grasping mind will get weaker, and your true nature, compassion, will be given a chance to emerge more and more strongly. The stronger and greater your compassion, the stronger and greater your fearlessness and confidence. So compassion reveals itself yet again as your greatest resource and your greatest protection. As Shantideva says:
>
>> Whosoever wishes to quickly afford protection
>> To both himself and others
>> Should practice that holy secret:
>> The exchange of self for others.

This holy secret of the practice of Tonglen is one that the mystic masters and saints of every tradition know; and living it and embodying it, with the abandon and fervor of true wisdom and true compassion, is what fills their lives with joy.[33]

The Practice

After you feel that you have connected to the godform and can sense it around you—a unity with it—breathe in brilliant white light; feel your energy expand, and an increase of love, compassion, and inner knowing. Hold for a few seconds and then exhale, feeling an expansion of this consciousness within you and the desire to share it with others. Perform this several times, allowing the feelings to build up within you.

Then, when you are ready, imagine the pain and suffering that exists in the world. Inhale, taking it into yourself; feel your inner self, the Thoth, or Wisdom energy within you, transform suffering into joy, happiness, and illumination. Exhale that out to the world.

Continue with this for several minutes, or a fixed amount of breaths.

When you are done, divest yourself of the godform by imagining that it shrinks down into your heart and, while still bright and vibrant, raises above your head and disappears into a point of light in the psychic center above your head.[34]

---

[33]Sogyal Rinpoche, *The Tibetan Book of Living and Dying* (San Francisco, CA: HarperCollins, 1993) 207.

[34]Kether or the Crown.

Perform a banishing ritual if you desire, or simply give the "Sign of Silence" or ring a bell to shift your focus back to the material world.

Practice this in the abstract; then, with time, work on assisting those close to you whom you are in sympathy with, then those with whom you are in disagreement, those who have injured you, and strangers.[35]

Communion
Gratitude and Grace with Friends and Enemies

Abraham broke bread and drank wine with the Righteous King of Peace, or Melchizedek. This custom became the basis of the Passover Feast and the later Christian Mass. The image is repeated in Christ's Last Supper, and again in the idea of the Round Table in Arthurian romances, and even in Knights Templar Freemasonry.[36] However, Melchizedek, or "The Righteous King," represents the highest of human development: the "Tzadek," or what is poorly translated as "Jewish Saint." This idea is similar to the Unknown Superiors of later lore, and to the *Bodhisattvas* of Buddhism. In astrology the planet Jupiter,[37] the expression of Chesed's energy, rules over the simple pleasures of life, as well as spiritual and material expansion, and celebrations.

This simple rite has its roots in antiquity[38] and connects

---

[35] Rinpoche, *op. cit.*, 201-8.

[36] See "The Order of the Knights Templars" in Jabez Richardson, *Richardson's Monitor of Free-Masonry* (Chicago, IL: Ezra A. Cook Publishers, 1975 ed.) 113-27.

[37] In Hebrew, the name for Jupiter is "Tzadek."

[38] A similar rite is found in the Tibetan Bön tradition. Bön claims

us to the Holy Ones who walk on Earth but whom we see not.

> One of the simplest and most complete magick ceremonies is the Eucharist. It consists of taking common things, transmuting them into things divine, and consuming them... **A Eucharist of some sort should most assuredly be consumed daily by every Magician, and he should regard it as the main substance of his magical life.** It is more important than any other magical ceremony, because it is a complete circle. The whole of the force expended is completely reabsorbed; yet the virtue is that vast gain represented by the abyss between Man and God.
>
> **The Magician becomes filled with God, fed upon God, intoxicated with God. Little by little his body will become purified by the internal lustrations of God; day by day his mortal frame, shedding its earthly elements, will become in very truth the Temple of the Holy Ghost. Day by day matter is replaced by Spirit, the human by the divine;** ultimately

---

three major influences, the oldest of which is from the area of Central Asia where modern Iran is located. This is significant for those looking for a common source behind many of Europe and Asia's esoteric teachings. See: Tenzin Wangyal Rinpoche, *Healing with Form, Energy and Light: The Five Elements in Tibetan Shamanism, Tantra, and Dzogchen* (Ithaca, NY: Snow Lion Publications, 2002). Sanskrit, the "Mother of Languages," has its roots in the Caucusus Mountains region, above modern Turkey. One scholar puts forth the premise that the Pharaonic period of Egypt began with missionaries from that region emigrating to Egypt.

the change will be complete; God manifest in flesh will be his name.[39]

The Common Meal

Communion rites, meals, and offerings also serve to bond people together. Here, the bonding is not limited to human beings, but to all the beings in the universe to whom we share a relationship. The underlying ideal of Chesed is often expressed in the number thirteen. Thirteen is significant in that it is the number of "achad," or "unity" in Hebrew, and the number of participants in a theurgic rite (as exemplified by the "Last Supper"). Thirteen can be reduced to four using theosophic reduction, thereby bringing the idea of "unity in diversity" full circle, as four is the number of Chesed. Here, the unity is a genuine and true unity, that reflects the function and purpose of each element, and not a contrived or forced unity that ignores essential differences or weaknesses.

Chesed is associated with the function of memory in qabalistic psychology. Memory is life, and in this domain we become free from the cycle of birth and death, because we remember our past lives, actions, and their consequences. This memory serves to guide us in making decisions that are in harmony with our fundamental desire to Become, and to help others in their unfoldment.

When working with the image of a cup or Grail we bring ourselves into unity with all that is, and especially our personal destiny. The Grail becomes the symbol of our receptivity to the *vocation* or service we are to perform in

---

[39] Aleister Crowley, *Magick: Book 4*, Second Edition (York Beach, ME: Samuel Weiser, Inc., 1997) 267-69. Emphasis in original.

the material world. In various schools of yoga, the disciple visualizes an image of their teacher in the center of their heart. In working with the Grail, do the same, visualizing it in the form that resonates best with your tradition: this can be a cup, vase, or any receptacle. Tradition states that a crystal or stone are excellent receptacles of force and light, and often appear in the Grail legends; even the Black Stone of the Kaaba which Gabriel gave to Abraham, or the dark crystal can be used.

Preliminary Work with the Grail

> Those who are [on the Grail] quest are like those who devote themselves to the Bodhisattva concept. In Buddhism, a Bodhisattva is one who vows never to re-enter Nirvana until "the last blade of grass" enters first... For the essence of the Grail quest is not to disappear into a never-never land of no return; our duty is to return bearing the gifts of regeneration and remembrance to every living creature. We become the Grail that others may drink; for to find the Grail is to become it.[40]

Visualize your chosen symbol in your heart and begin the meditation. Your physical heartbeat and breathing may resonate with it, or you may feel it burning inside of you, activating your psychic heart. This is a test of your ability (or better, of your desire) to be a candidate for the transmission of the Inner Mysteries. It is an act of self-consecration and

---

[40] John Matthews, ed., *At the Table of the Grail* (London: Arkana Books, 1984) 126-7.

it is equivalent to knocking at the door of Inner Initiation, and announcing that you are ready to be instructed in your Path of Service—and to be a link in the visible and invisible chain reaching back to Melki-Tzedek. This initiatic chain of transmission is constructed with many links of which only a minority are incarnate on earth at any time. This invisible and visible chain is the Universal Church of which von Eckartshausen wrote in *The Cloud of Unknowing*. All authentic traditions and servants draw their authority from being an active part of this chain. In doing so, we realize that we are not alone in our work (although it may seem that way at times), but are supported by many seen and unseen helpers when the need arises. The "burning heart" is the stimulation of your psychic heart, and a sign that you have been "accepted" by the Inner Masters. The most important Master, however, is not outside of you, but is in truth your own Higher Self, even if it may take the form of "someone else."[41]

The Symbolic Table

The Table is a significant symbol: it acts as both table and altar. It is a place of reception and sacrifice. This is especially amplified when linked to the notion of the banquet or feast. In the Grail Legends, each time the Grail appears the Knights are all sitting at the Round Table. Like the Biblical "manna in the desert" of the Old Testament (which tasted like the food each desired most), the Grail actualizes for each Knight what they most deeply desire in the secret

---

[41] Jean Dubuis, *The Philosophers of Nature Qabala Course*, Lesson 15 (Wheaton, IL: Triad Publishing, 2000) 4.

place of their heart. This also suggests the transmutative power of Christ's blood, which according to legend was collected in the Grail by Joseph of Arimathea at the time of the Crucifixion.

In the texts of the Grail Quest there are five tables:

The Table of the Last Supper where Jesus, surrounded by his twelve disciples, accomplished the sacrifice through bread and wine.

The Table of Pentecost where the Holy Spirit descends on the Disciples.

The Table of Joseph of Arimathea who was the first Guardian of the Grail.

The Round Table around which Arthur's companions are assembled.

The Table of the Mass, which is a synthesis and extension into the popular consciousness of all of the preceding Tables and their power of community.

In the early Roman Church, there were two altars, symbolic of the two functions of the "table" as both that of sacrifice and celebration.

Preliminary Work with the Table

In this exercise, we are going to visualize the Table. We can use any of the tables listed above. Many start with the Round Table; while this is symbolically easiest, it is important to work through each of the tables, meditating on their significance, commonalities, and uniqueness. Our companions seated with us and the Christ as God on His Throne in the East is ideal for the Round Table, or seated in the center when working with the Last Supper. Re-read the appropriate Scripture passages, and sections of the Grail legends, when working with these images. During this exercise we shall humbly ask to be instructed about our purpose here on earth. A purpose or destiny—a karmic unfoldment, if you will—that is common to all the Disciples, companions, or Knights seated with us (who are our different energies and potentialities). We shall ask for a benediction and investiture for ourself and our "associates," fully aware that this initiates a breakthrough on our path that will carry us forward.[42]

Rituals such as these are performed with a great deal of visualization, and as such can be done with or without the physical tools of bread, wine, and salt. Anything that is at hand can be used, and if even water is not available, the entire process can be imagined in rich detail, and still be magnificently efficient.

1. Perform relaxation and breathing exercises, focusing on your heart. Imagine a brilliant glow of golden light from your heart forming a sphere, which radiates its warmth and light to a larger sphere or space around you. Allow this space to increase to about nine feet all around you.
2. Give an offering of thanks and sincere gratitude for your spiritual teachers, the tradition you are in, and the line of teachers that have made that tradition

---

[42]Modification of Jean Dubuis, *The Philosophers of Nature Qabala Course*, Lesson 17 (Wheaton, IL: Triad Publishing, 2000) 6.

possible up to the present day. This can be a simple visualization of its principal deities and personalities, accompanied by robed and hooded "unknowns"—both adepts such as the "Unknown Superiors" and students who have sacrificed for the Tradition—forming the chain that leads up to you. Surround yourself with them and invite them to be present with you in your act of Inner Communion. Include archangels, angels, the Elemental Sovereigns, and their retinues, as well.[43]

3. Give an offering of thanks to your friends, family, neighbors, and others who have assisted you in being where you are today. Visualize them and invite them to accompany you in your act of inner communion.

4. Give an offering of thanks to, and invite, the strangers you've encountered, and the many people you have not met; include your enemies, and the shells of the astral region who wander in pain, the chaotic forces of the *qlippoth*, and any spirit in need.

5. Sanctify your bread and wine, or meal offering.

6. See those you've invited participate in it with you, receiving to the best of their ability the Illumination

---

[43] Consider this in light of the following:

> Be aware then first of the origins of the Table and the wonder and power of He whose table it is at which you aspire to sit. Then be aware of your companions, visible and invisible, human and non-human who also serve. The Table is a symbol of the corporate nature of any man's service and in one way it could be said that the Grail does not manifest until all are sitting at the Table Round.

From: Gareth Knight, *Experience of the Inner Worlds* (York Beach, ME: Samuel Weiser, Inc., 1993) 145.

they seek.
7. Save a small portion of the bread and wine, or food—a few crumbs will do, as it is the energy contained within it, and not the amount, that matters. Cast it outside for the astral shells, Elementals, and demons, imagining that they receive the blessing and Illumination they seek and need.
8. Thank your guests for attending, and release or send them on their way. This may be done using the Rose+Cross[44] or any other suitable means (although the Rose+Cross is exceptionally well fitted for this particular blessing).

Demonic Guests

The inclusion of demonic, chaotic, and qlippothic entities into our retinue of guests is important. By recognizing them as being part of ourselves and our evolution, they fulfill a dual role of providing a great deal of potential energy in material work and reflecting the inner work we need to do. For many modern esoteric groups, there is an outright fear of negative forces, coupled with forgetting that there is really

---

[44]The Rose+Cross is performed by comfortably extending your arm and, with the first two fingers, drawing a line from the height of your forehead to about your solar plexus, then drawing a cross arm from about the height of your left shoulder to your right shoulder, while pronouncing the Divine Name "Yeheshua." A circle is then drawn connecting the arms of the cross, starting at the left arm, moving to the top, then right, to the bottom, and completing the circle, while pronouncing the Divine Name "Yehovasha." This is all done in one fluid action, with the cross being drawn in the air in front of you and away from your body.

no such thing as a "negative," only a virtue or strength that is overdone, and applied to the point of excess.

By including them in our acts of thanks and gratitude, we weaken their destructive impact on our life and begin to make friends with them. They become our useful helpers and we become their guides.

The negative entities associated with Chesed are *Ga'ashekelah*, or "those who break things apart." Expressions of Chesed's mercy gone to the extreme and turned sour include: greed, debauchery, and an endless inflation of self. This is often done by forming relationships that are parasitical and not designed to liberate either party from ignorance. A more common expression is the collapse or outright deconstruction of boundaries, so that the wave of pathology associated with human activity becomes commonplace and accepted. The abuse of power and doing things because they *can* be done—rather than that they *should* be done—by those in power, is an example of the potential destructiveness of Chesed's influence, when the understanding of "right relations" and "right actions" are ignored.

Some students may find it difficult, if not impossible, to believe that they are ready to perform such meditations. However, like all limitations, such thoughts exist only in the mind of whomever holds them. To imagine oneself as perfect, as a fully illuminated being, as a *Supérieur Inconnu*, bestowing blessings upon those around you and becoming a Being of Light, Life, Love, Liberty, and Law, is completely natural.

In fact, the technique is not advanced at all, but completely consistent with the most fundamental of esoteric principles. When we seek to create some level of change in our outer environment, we have available to us the technique of creative visualization. In using this method, we imagine the desired object or condition, complete and fully realized. We are told to think of the goal and not the steps. Let the subconscious (the Cosmic, nature, or what have you) take care of the details. The same is true here. By focusing on the goal, we stimulate and awaken within ourselves corresponding qualities. Slowly, over time, and in a manner often unnoticed, we look back and realize that we have grown inwardly, and are coming closer to realizing the goal of Perfect Illumination as a permanent state of being.

Conclusion

In closing, there are no better words than those of one modern Rosicrucian authority:[45]

> The most important quality to be made permanent in the disciple's equipment, after the meditative and contemplative contact has been fully established, is that of spiritual militancy. This may be questioned, but I cannot retract. I would reemphasize it, and from another aspect. We have heard the word of peace spoken, with all the variations of human rhetoric, when there is no peace. On the contrary, we live virtually in a time of war [1937]. The world atmosphere in which we live is a militant one. We may close our eyes to it in our prayers and meditations, but we can no more shut out the world atmosphere

---

[45] Andrea, *The Mystic Path, op. cit.*, 161.

of militancy than we can cease to breathe. And if our Karma is bound up with the world Karma, we share it and have a responsibility in it. But this surely does not mean that the disciple must share in the militant tendencies of the world? No, not necessarily; but on his own level of life and in his own sphere of action and service, he must have aggressive and dominant faculties of a similar nature if he is to leave any mark of the way he has gone for those who would achieve now and those who hope to achieve in the future.[46]

---

[46]For those new to the Hermetic Path, we might end with this paragraph instead:

> But now it is time to enter into the adventure and become one in the royal, golden, occult chain of the tradition of the sons of Hermes: for which there only remains for us— and thus we come to the end—to repeat these words of the second Rosicrucian manifesto: "Anyone who comes looking for us simply out of curiosity, will never find us. But if his will truly and in fact is to inscribe himself in the registry of our fraternity, we, who judge by thought, will fulfill our promises to him. We do not divulge the place of our residence, because thoughts, united to the real will of reader, are capable of letting us know him, and him us." [Evola, *op. cit.*, 216.]

Summary

1. The Qabalistic Tree of Life has been the central working symbol in Western esotericism for nearly one thousand years.

2. The various levels, or "spheres," of the Tree of Life correspond to the various levels of the human psyche, body, the planets, and levels of consciousness.

3. As one progresses on the Path of Becoming, their consciousness becomes progressively more integrated and expansive.

4. Exterior initiation is used to stimulate this progressive integration and expansion as well as to suggest what lies ahead.

5. Each of the levels of the Tree has a name given to it corresponding to various levels of interior initiation, each with its own tasks to assist in further progress.

6. Interior initiation is genuine and permanent evolution of consciousness.

7. The level of Chesed corresponds to the title Adeptus Exemptus, whose practices are to develop mercy, compassion, and generosity on all levels.

8. One who is an Adeptus Exemptus on the inner level of initiation is similar to the Bodhisattva of Buddhism.

9. By imagining ourselves as already perfect and complete, and assisting in the evolution of others, we are able to

realize that the stages of development are also artificial constructs, and an aspect of duality.

10. By imagining ourselves as already perfect and complete we can further express and bring to fruition those qualities to a greater degree in our daily life.

11. The Tree of Life is a tool for expressing those qualities in a systematic manner.

12. Bringing everything into our Path of Becoming, and sharing our illumination with everyone—even if imagined—helps us to better express our perfect and complete nature, while seeing all things as both illusions and life's lessons.

Appendix

Z.1 Document of the Golden Dawn

[The following is taken from Israel Regardie, *The Golden Dawn* (St. Paul, MN: Llewellyn Publications, 1986) 330.]

THE GENERAL EXORDIUM

The Speech in the Silence:
The Words against the Son of Night;
The Voice of Thoth before the Universe in the presence of the eternal Gods:
The Formulas of Knowledge:
The Wisdom of Breath:
The Radix of Vibration;
The Shaking of the Invisible:
The Rolling Asunder of the Darkness:
The Becoming Visible of Matter:
The Piercing of the Coils of the Stooping Dragon:
The Breaking forth of the Light:
All these are in the Knowledge of Tho-oth.

THE PARTICULAR EXORDIUM

At the ending of the Night: At the Limits of the Light: Tho-oth stood before the Unborn Ones of Time!
Then was formulated the Universe:
Then came for the Gods thereof:
The Æons of the Bornless Beyond:
Then was the Voice vibrated:

Then was the Name declared.
At the Threshold of the Entrance,
Between the Universe and the Infinite,
In the Sign of the Enterer, stood Tho-oth,
As before him were the Æons proclaimed.
In Breath did he vibrate them:
In Symbols did he record them:
For betwixt the Light and the Darkness did he
  stand.

The *Particular Exordium* is most commonly used, although they may be used together.

Part II

Khamael's Spear

~

An Esoteric Response

to

War & Terrorism

Monograph Overview

- Current Affairs: A World in Crisis
- Group Mind, Group Soul, and How They are Influenced
- Three Factors in Occult Work: Practical Exercises to Change Our World

Introduction

This monograph is to instruct the reader in the theoretical and technical aspects of understanding current events focusing on terrorism and violence in the Middle East from an esoteric viewpoint, with emphasis on practical occult actions that can be taken to assist in creating a world focused on peace and spiritual well being. A careful reading of the material will show that the techniques are easily adaptable to other scenarios as well.

After reading this monograph, some readers may object to the notion of using psychic and occult techniques to affect world affairs, implying that it is some form of manipulation. To this we say: you are right. It *is* manipulation, and for the good of all concerned. Manipulation is constantly taking place, and its more grievous applications go unnoticed, but not un-felt. Given the threats civilization faces, would it be better to sit by and do nothing? Would it be better to allow the forces of hate and destruction to continue their march into the Holy Sanctuary of the human soul?

Make no doubt about it, war is about killing—and it is far better to kill an idea than a human being. War is the single most traumatic event that can be foisted upon the human psyche. Its scars are deep and lasting.

> The soldier in combat is trapped within this tragic Catch-22. If he overcomes his resistance to killing and kills an enemy soldier in close combat, he will be forever burdened with blood guilt, and if he elects not to kill, then the blood guilt of his fallen comrades and the shame of his profession, nation, and cause lie upon him. He is damned if he does, and damned if he doesn't.[1]

Think of what we ask here as an act of Mercy.

Theoretical Background

The application of spiritual and occult forces to attempt to influence world events is nothing new. In recent history occult practices were utilized by British ritualists to reinforce the health and safety of Great Britain during the Second

---

[1] Lt. Col. Dave Grossman, *On Killing: The Psychological Cost of Learning to Kill in War and Society* (New York: Little, Brown, & Co., 1996) 87.

World War; French occultists resurrected at least one of their ancient magical orders, the Elus Cohen, during this period as well. Many occultists risked their lives to keep, preserve, maintain, and even expand their spiritual teachings during the dark periods before, during, and after the war years of 1939 to 1945. Some of the directions from that period are available today; in conjunction with other ritualistic material, both qabalistic and more general, this monograph will demonstrate how each student of practical esotericism can assist in bringing safety to their land, peace to the world, and an end to religiously justified and inspired terrorism.

For the United States of America, the messages of September 11th were manifold, but can be summed up in several points:

1. The United States and Europe have been at war for nearly 25 years with terrorist organizations and states whose goal is to see the destruction of Israel and the United States. From 1981 to 2001 there were 7,581 terrorist attacks worldwide which killed and injured a significant number of people.

2. America has traded its culture for consumerism, and from its mass consumption has become dependent on unstable sources of energy for its continued rush into the economic, environmental, cultural, and spiritual abyss.

3. The majority of the world, outside of Western Europe, Japan, Australia, New Zealand, and North America, are difficult and at times very dangerous places where life is hard, short, and often brutal by Western ideals and standards of ethics and morality.

4. There are forces within the United States at both extremes of the political chasm that seek to take advantage of this unstable situation for their own advancement and without genuine concern for the greater good or the rule of law.

5. Most importantly, pretending that the points made above do not exist doesn't make them go away. As much as we might like it to be otherwise, we do not live on an island anymore.

This leads us to a final point, and to the purpose of this paper: while many want the war in Iraq to end quickly, as it is a drain on our national treasure, talent, and morale, it must be clear to our readers that the withdrawing of American forces will not end the war. Militant Islamic forces, supported by a complacent or terrified Islamic majority, will not stop until their goal is reached.

The Group Mind and Group Soul

Groups, from the smallest family unit to nations and worlds, form collective attitudes or mindsets, composed of values and notions of what is important, right, or wrong, mostly focusing on human relations and spiritual ideas. As collective groups form communities, and the rule of law takes precedence over rule of emotions, customs, and chaos, these laws become the written codes whereupon civilizations are established.

In doing so, the raw power of the individual and the collective is slowly reigned in and kept in check. Trials take the place of revenge killings; evidence, procedure, debate, and reason take the place of lynching, mob "justice," or "drum head" court-martials.

A critical point must be made here and understood well if the urgency of this work is to have any meaning.

For the psychologist, emotional force is the primary motivator in human activities. For the occultist, emotional force is the primary force of their being; it is THE energy that creates conditions and events that seek to manifest on the material level. This force, once mobilized, tincts or colors everything it touches, either bringing it into alignment with its purpose or pushing it away. This force reaches beyond the limits of the individual into the collective consciousness (or more accurately unconsciousness) of every group that person is involved with, even the nation and the world to some degree. When combined with the emotional force of others, this focused and specific energy can dominate the consciousness of the mass of human beings who exist in a sort of "dreamland" of psychic and material vibrations, and whose sense of identity is tied to physical existence.

This works in both a positive evolutionary manner—the manner we are seeking to use it—as well as in a negative manner, as we are seeing in the form of Islamic Fascism and its terrorist spawn.

It is critical that this parasitical force be stripped from Islam if Islam is to survive. It is also important that it be stripped from the Arab people if they are to survive and grow into greater self-government and personal responsibility.

> The occultist believes that emotion is a force...that in the case of the ordinary man radiates out from him in all directions, forming a magnetic field; but

> in the case of the trained occultist it can be concentrated into a beam and directed. Supposing you are to concentrate your whole attention upon a single feeling, inhibiting all else, you will have achieved a pure emotional state... All the life-force coming into your soul will therefore flow in this single subdivision...the concentration will be terrific, but will only be achieved at a terrific price... Such (developed) concentration is good for one purpose, and one purpose only. We can concentrate on healing or destruction, but we cannot work both simultaneously; neither can we readily change from one to the other... Momentum has to be checked and worked up again before reversal of spin can take place.[2]

From the above paragraph, it is clear that for the Middle East to grow into a self-confident, democratic nation—or at least a moderate dictatorship heading towards democracy—the current direction of force must be stopped, or contained until it burns out. There will be a pause, a silence or rest of seeming inactivity, and then the momentum in a new direction will be undertaken. However, the greater the spin towards chaos and destruction, the greater the period of rest, and the slower the movement towards evolution.

Simultaneously, by realizing that we in the developed countries of the West (the United States in particular) have a role to play in this dysfunctional and deadly relationship, we can begin to focus more of our attention on solutions that weaken the ties to unstable regions, resources, and ideologies,

---

[2]Dion Fortune, *Psychic Self-Defense*, New Edition (York Beach, ME: Weiser Books, 2001) 137-8.

at home and abroad.

Groups create, sustain, and grow a collective consciousness or identity (Group Mind) and a collective power or subconscious base (Group Soul). Combined they form an artificial creation, very much like a giant human being, known as an *egregore*, or "Watcher." These *Watchers*, also known as Guardians, are very real, and very influential to all that comes under their domain. They can only be changed from within, but they can be contained by other egregores, in the same fashion that one individual can prevent another from doing harm or walking into traffic without looking. One person can impact another person, or a collective entity can impact a collective entity, without really changing the other's essential identity or function. They simply stop it from moving in a particular direction.

In her work, *The Cosmic Doctrine*, Dion Fortune states:

> It is necessary, if you are to understand the deeper implications of occultism, that you should see that darkness leads through twilight into dawn, and day leads twilight to darkness.
>
> Good and evil may be conceived of as areas of light and shadow through which a spinning ring evolved, and evil has its work to do as well as good. The God of Light and the God of Darkness are but the actions of the Right and Left Hand of the Father. The Right-Hand gives that which is to be, and the Left-Hand takes away that which has been. The Right sends out into manifestation and the Left beckons back again; but you, looking as in a mirror, call Right

Left, and Left Right.[3]

Fortune states that a premature attempt at returning to the Source or center of a creative vortex—i.e., God—can generate an imperfect creation that is parasitical to life. These kinds of parasites, as we have stated, arise on the physical, emotional, mental, and spiritual levels.

When they attach themselves to a sympathetic host, such as an individual, neurosis and psychotic behaviors result. When they attach themselves to a group, such as a family, dysfunctional behaviors emerge, as well as conflict when an attempt at rebalance is made. When they attach themselves to larger mass relationships, periods of social unrest occur that often result in bloodshed until the parasite is removed, or if the host can no longer support it because of illness or death.

In traditional settings, it is the purpose of exorcism to remove the influence of these parasites and restore a person or place to balance.

Understanding the nature of group dynamics, particularly when applied to war, is also important for, as we have shown, human beings have an instinctual abhorrence for killing other human beings. Extensive conditioning is required to overcome this inhibition. When we examine why men in combat kill, we see that it is due to four reasons, all group related. People kill because of (1) regard for their comrades; (2) respect or fear of their leaders; (3) concern for their personal reputation with both; and (4) a need to contribute to the success of the group.[4]

---

[3]Dion Fortune, *The Cosmic Doctrine*, New Edition (York Beach, ME: Weiser Books, 2000) 182.

[4]Grossman, *op. cit.*, 89-90.

The Goal: Staying Apolitical

We want to change attitudes and feelings, to create an environment where positive and life-sustaining philosophies and actions will take place. This is the goal. It is broad, it is general, and it is not "fuzzy"; however, in that it allows for human choice and free will, it remains very clear that totalitarianism, excessive restrictions, and unlawfulness by individuals, groups, or governments at home or abroad will not be tolerated.

This work is to endorse and support the ideal, letting each find the means of expression within themselves, as individuals, ethnic groups, religions, or nation states.

The Notion of Justice

Modern esoteric and spiritual movements talk a great deal about the underlying unity of things. Comparisons with Einstein's search for a Unified Field Theory or examples drawn from contemporary quantum physics are often used to illustrate a point. While we are told that this unity is ever-present, though, it seems that most are at a loss for experiencing it. The kind of experience many will talk about is of a cosmic "oneness," or consciousness. It is this very sense of connectedness that draws people closer to each other and makes the act of war more difficult. To kill another requires that we feel (and often physically be) distant and separate from them. It is hard to kill someone when you are looking them in the eyes, or feel them to be a peer or equal. Yet, we see terrorists not only killing up close and very personally, but killing indiscriminately, often killing themselves in the process. A suicide bomber needs to feel very disconnected from those he or she will kill; even more importantly, they must feel disconnected from themselves as well. It is for this reason that those who have intellectual deficits are specifically targeted, groomed, and manipulated into being suicide killers.

> The link between distance and ease of aggression is not a new discovery. It has long been understood that there is a direct relationship between the empathic and physical proximity of the victim, and the resultant difficulty and trauma of the kill... At the far end of the spectrum are bombing and artillery, which are often used to illustrate the relative ease of long-range killing. As we draw towards the near end of the spectrum, we begin to realize that the resistance to killing becomes increasingly more intense...and killing with the bare hands...becomes almost unthinkable. Yet even this is not the end...when we address the macabre region at the extreme end of the scale, where sex and killing intermingle.[5]

Human ideas of justice are constantly seeking to perfect themselves, and in a shadowy fashion to become closer to the ideal and function of Universal Justice. In ancient Egypt, the goddess Maat was the supreme ideal. Justice, or Balance, everything being "exactly as it should be," was the philosophical basis for Egyptian theocracy. In Maat, Egypt was seen as a mirror of the invisible, and a perfect reflection of cosmic order and harmony. It is no wonder

---

[5] *Ibid.* 97-98.

that the Hermetic axiom—"as above, so below; as below, so above"—should arise there.

For Hermeticists, wellness, health, happiness, and illumination are seen as expressions of perfect balance and harmony. The removal of obstacles rather than the addition of qualities or quantities is the object of this work.

In Qabala, the mysterious sphere of *Daäth* represents supreme justice, balance, and cosmic order.

Daäth represents a point at which the perfect ideas of justice, law, and equilibrium are synthesized. It is a perfect unification of the entire Tree of Life in a single point, in which divine wisdom, love, and power are united. Within each of us stands the great Tree of Life in microcosm, wherein Daäth contains the key that allows us to unlock the inner knowledge of our self. It contains the Record or the *Book of Nature* (or *Life*) where we may find written the sum of our experiences and how they affect our evolution.

For the average qabalist, little is done with Daäth, and with the exception of the most experienced worker, Daäth should be approached with a fair degree of caution.

Meditation on Daäth should only be undertaken by less experienced students when they approach it with the intention of bringing their human ideas of justice into greater harmony with cosmic or *universal* justice. In this instance, the symbol used is the balanced scales, the red ostrich feather of Maat, or the two combined as seen in the Egyptian *Book of the Dead*.

> Therefore it must be emphasized that meditations on Daäth, unless very carefully decided on beforehand and directed, are not very safe, except when they are just approached with a view of helping the human

idea of Justice when such a thing is necessary for balancing up the development of the soul...to know that the Supreme Balance may be in some manner approached in order to show how the balance of the smaller human world works out.[6]

So then we must ask, "What is so dangerous about Daäth?" It is illuminating to replace the Hebrew word with its translation and ask, rather, "What is so dangerous about *Knowledge?*"

The knowledge Daäth brings is the experience on some level of greater integration. It shakes out the useless and outworn, bringing a greater realization of the mind of God. This brings us to the Experience of Eternity.[7]

However, Daäth is present in all levels; it cannot be avoided entirely, simply viewed "through a glass darkly" rather than head-on. One of the places we experience this profound concentration of justice, power, and wisdom is in the astral realm, especially the vibration of the invisible immediately influencing the material world, or (as it is called in Qabala) the Sphere of Yesod.

Daäth and Yesod share an especially close relationship. The focal point of Daäth pulses a vibration that must increase in density if it is to manifest materially. For this to happen, Yesod (the lower astral) modifies the pulse so that it is relatively harmonious with Earth's aura. Since each of us has our own "Yesod" as we have our own "Daäth," we can think of it as a form of subconscious filtering so that the

---

[6]Fortune, *The Mystical Qabala, op. cit.*, 331.
[7]See: Mark Stavish, "The Portæ Lucis Method of Jean Dubuis" at hermeticinstitute.org.

ideas and energies can be integrated. Here again, this also applies to groups, nations, movements, etc., all of which have their own Tree of Life complete with all the levels, including Daäth.

Experienced ritualists will also recognize that each time the Archangels of the Quarters are invoked (strengthening the etheric connection between the visible and invisible realms), Daäth—a unity between the cosmic mind and human mind—is to some degree increased.

In short, all ritual work aimed at unity will invoke aspects of the divine mind, manifesting power, wisdom, and justice in and through us. This can be directed to work greater social good, but it must be clear that it will always have a disruptive effect on the individual and collective consciousness as previous conceptions are jettisoned, and the new impulse is integrated. This disruption is, however, minimized by consciously addressing the issues presented rather than allowing them to fester and explode, infecting the entire personality or society.

Dispersing the Clouds of War

If one is to deal with an enemy, it is important to understand that enemy. For us, that means the mass of destructive energy that is gathered around the world, but which presently finds its focus and outlet primarily in the Middle East and through the Islamic faith. It is important to separate the expression from the energy, or the "gasoline from the motorcar," if you will. While various expressions of evil exist, they can be seen in three primary ways:

Sin. Sin is human error—a mistake, and while it may do harm, there was no direct intention to do harm. It is as the word means, "to miss the point," to misunderstand, to be in error.

Excess. Excess is similar to sin, in that a good thing or idea becomes the prominent filter through which all other ideas and actions are expressed. Simply put, "too much of a good thing" becomes a deficit.

Evil. Here we are talking about destruction for its own sake. This may have two forms: unconscious force—a blind rage—and conscious decisions to destroy.

> The student must carefully distinguish between what the occultist calls positive and negative evil... Positive evil is a force which is moving against the current of evolution; negative evil is simply the opposition of an inertia which has not yet been overcome, or of a momentum which has not yet been neutralized... It then follows that the solution to the problem of evil and its eradication from the world is not to be achieved through its suppression, cutting off, or destruction, but through its compensation and consequent absorption back into the Sphere (Sephirah) whence it came... Whenever we make ourselves the channel for any pure force, that is to say any force which is single and undiluted by ulterior motives and secondary considerations, we find that there is a river in spate behind us—the stream of the corresponding Sephirothic or Qlippothic forces that are finding a channel through us. It is this that gives

the single-minded zealot his abnormal power.[8]

The majority of human beings commit errors which fall under the first two points. Given the right opportunity and emotional environment, they will most often make the right decision. Human concerns, fears, pettiness, and other issues of underdevelopment in their consciousness affect their judgment. When sufficient frustration, anger, and negative human emotions accumulate, we enter into the realm of unconscious evil. Here, the blind force of destruction seeks an outlet, and like fire seeking fuel, goes to wherever it can find an outlet. This raw force is found in the individual and collective consciousness of groups, no matter what their size; similar to "spirits" in talismanic and planetary workings, it can and must be directed if it is to have any long-term effect. It must also be continually fed to be kept at sufficient frenzy where the rational mind is limited in its ability to regain control of the individual or collective organism.

Once given a fever pitch, this blind rage is then directed into action by conscious evil. This comes from the very top: the few who understand human psycho-spirituality and who seek to do destruction for its own sake. Even when their original ideals may be good, these leaders at some point become more concerned with the destruction of their enemies (real or perceived) and those who would even simply disagree with their vision, rather than the positive aspects of the vision itself.

This is important: For the individual and collective mind to be attracted to and directed by conscious evil, there must be a "positive vision" that holds their attention which

---

[8]Fortune, *The Mystical Qabala, op. cit.*, 281-83.

is then manipulated and turned against them and others.

If the emotional energy that conscious evil needs is removed from it, then it no longer has the power-base required to make significant impact in the world.

For this reason, a significant part of our work is aimed at:

1. Disconnecting the leadership from its power base.
2. Creating a healthy psychic environment to prevent or limit the influence of destructive energies.
3. Creating a healthy psychic environment at home that will stimulate spiritual awakening, active participation in this work, and that will strengthen our defenses against foreign and domestic forces that would seek to undermine our way of life.

Three Factors in Occult Work

Three primary factors are at work in any occult operations:

1. **Hypnotic suggestion and affirmation.** This may also include telepathy if the work is for someone other than the Operator. Hypnotic suggestion need not be in a deep trance state—the majority of the time it is not. This can be seen on the religious level in the utilization of specific and regular prayers. On the political level it can be seen in the chanting of slogans, use of catch phrases, and media "sound bites."
2. **Reinforcement of the suggestion by ritualistic means and invocation of invisible agencies.** On the religious level this is seen by weekly and daily

worship and collective holidays. On the political level it is by linking "God" to the "cause," such as in making the desired political goal the "will of God."

3. **Reinforcement of the suggestion by physical means, such as with a symbol or, more potently, a point of physical contact, such as a talisman or "sacred object."** On a religious level, this can be seen in the communion wafer that links the individual to the community and the community to Christ. On the political level, this can be seen in the "Blood Flag" of Naziism. Each Nazi banner was brought into contact with this banner, held sacred because it was used in the failed Munich *Putsch* and held the blood of the "martyrs" who fell that day. Propaganda in the form of mass media, images, advertising, etc., is the most common means of using this point.

How Many Does It Take?

A common question, especially among new students, is "How many people does it take to make a ritual work?" This is especially amplified when talking about larger projects that affect many people or a wide area. In truth it takes very few. This is often not believed—and because it is not believed, it doesn't work. However, if we look to both mundane and esoteric authorities we see that most social change has been done by a handful of people. Jesus had twelve disciples around him, and another sixty or so on a regular basis, with another sixty or seventy irregularly after that. There were only nine Templars in the founding years of the Knights Templar. There were only eight original

Rosicrucians mentioned in the *Fama Fraternitatis*. The Hermetic Order of the Golden Dawn had approximately three hundred members pass through it during its original phase, and of those, only one hundred reached the Second Order (Adeptus Minor Grade), whose techniques are so well known today and are the basis for nearly every magical order in the West. Dion Fortune stated that during the Second World War only seven people were needed to carry out an effective occult defense of Great Britain.[9] Numbers don't matter: they take care of themselves if there is confidence, dedication, perseverance, and regularity among those who are doing the work.

Preliminary Practice

Generating Good Will

This is the most important practice of all, and can be done alone or preliminary to the practices that follow.

1. Sit in a chair, back straight, feet apart, hands resting unclasped, palms down, on your thighs.
2. Breathe slowly and deeply through your nose. Hold for as long as comfortable, and then exhale slowly out of your nose. Hold your breath out for a few seconds.
3. Inhale again, and repeat the process given above for two to four minutes, allowing yourself to relax.
4. Focus your attention on your crown, or the area about

---

[9] Dion Fortune (introduction & commentary by Gareth Knight), *The Magical Battle of Britain* (Bradford on Avon [UK]: Golden Gates, 1993).

6-12 inches above your head. Imagine a brilliant sphere of white light centered there, so bright that it illuminates everything around you, and bathes you in brilliant light.
5. Breathe as instructed above for a minute or two, feeling a subtle pressure on top of your head increase.
6. Imagine a ray of light coming from the sphere and descending into your head, and from there down into your heart.
7. Imagine a brilliant sphere of golden light forming around your heart, warming it and extending outward some distance from your body.
8. Continue breathing as instructed above, and feel the heat, light, and love from your heart extend beyond your body, up to an area about six feet around you.
9. Continue breathing as instructed, simply focusing on the idea of generating compassion, mercy, and love, and allowing it to flow out from your heart, filling the space around you.
10. Continue, allowing the energy to expand, visualizing it surrounding and penetrating the area of the Middle East, with focus on areas where violence is strongest. Feel compassion flow from you, into everyone and everything there.
11. Continue breathing as instructed, allowing your breath and compassion to expand, grow, and saturate the world.
12. When you are done, breathe slowly and deeply several times, stand up, and declare verbally that the session is over for today.

Mountain of the Philosophers

Sit and breathe as prescribed above for several minutes. Generate compassion and allow it to fill the area around you. When this is complete, move on to the following.

Visualize a vast mountain[10] with its peak covered in clouds. A stone wall surrounds it, with an opening facing you. You pass through the gate and enter into the mountain. After passing down a long hallway, the first room you enter is the Library. The Library is the symbol of the Archives of Nature, the Astral Mirror, or the collective unconscious. This is important, as it is where the information, as well as instinctual power, resides.

The Library

The Library is a vast room with windows opening to the night sky, where a full moon hangs low over the horizon. In fact, the power of the moon is everywhere, and if one were to look out any window the moon would be present there as well. Imagine a chair, table, and rows of shelves heading into infinity. Let this take any design you wish. In the center of the library, between the rows of shelves in the main aisle in the main foyer, is a large spiral staircase. This staircase leads up past the ceiling, into another room. A soft golden light can be seen around the edges of the entranceway as it leads into the room above. This is a large staircase, as the library itself is vast and has a massive ceiling and several balconies around the edge of the room. Ladders on

---

[10]This technique is heavily modified from the original presented in *The Magical Battle of Britain*, op. cit.

rollers are attached to the bookshelves to allow access to the highest volumes, and ancient covers of bark, leather, metal, and papyrus line the shelves.

Here you will meet your Inner Self in the form of the Keeper of Records. It may be Thoth, Ezra, Azrael, or any of the Recording Angels of the ancient lines.

Imagine also that others are in this library with you. They are learning and preparing for the work ahead, that they may undertake it in full awareness and consciousness, knowing fully that their actions are recorded for posterity. As we read the records in this room of those who have gone before us, so will others read the records of what we have done.

Inner Sanctum

The Inner Sanctum is the seat of consciousness both human and divine. It connects to all levels of being, save the material. After one or two weeks, during which you have developed the image of the Library to a comfortable level, walk to the staircase and proceed to climb it. Notice that it twists clockwise as you ascend. Walk to the top and enter into a new room. This is the Inner Sanctum. You are halfway up the Mountain of the Philosophers.

The Inner Sanctum is vast and cavernous. In the center is a large Rose+Cross, golden with a single red rose in the center. Living green foliage adorns it, and the soft scent of roses fills the room. The altar is made of black marble, triangular, and three feet tall, with each side three feet in length. This is the symbol of manifestation. The apex of the triangle points towards the back of the room, making the base face the entranceway where you have entered from below.

The colors of the prism can be seen flashing around the cross. Around the edges of the Inner Sanctum are seven small alcoves; a presence can be sensed in each of them. The strength of each presence is reflected in the strength of its corresponding flashing color around the Rose+Cross.

A prayer stool is several feet from the altar, and allows you to kneel comfortably. Rest your arms on the soft cloth-covered shelf before you. Close your eyes. Relax. Feel the presence of others in the room with you. Each has come to do the same work as you. Find confidence in your comradeship and spiritual union.

Here, ask, pray, visualize—whatever it is you see fit to do—that divine power, compassion, and wisdom fill your heart and mind. Ask that this divine virtue go forth and bring peace to the land. Then, extend this presence to the Middle East, to areas of conflict and fighting. Imagine the light flooding the land, comforting those who have experienced loss, bringing peace to those who are at war. Focus your attention on places of worship. Fill them with the brilliant light of the divine presence. Imagine that holy men are preaching peace and not war. If there are exceptionally bellicose speakers, imagine that their voices are not heard. Their audiences walk away; they are unseen, unheard, and their message of hate is ineffective. See them simply fade away, and witness a presence of divine compassion and wisdom take their place.

Tower of Vision

The Tower of Vision gives elevation on the astral planes. To see farther we must raise higher, where the winds and rain blow stronger. Here the tower represents our increased vision as a result of our repeated efforts to be of service. It offers greater vision or knowledge, but with that knowledge comes greater responsibility. Wait in the Inner Sanctum until you receive a sign of your readiness to ascend to the Tower of Vision. Once the sign is received, return to the spiral staircase. Now you will also see an adjacent ascending staircase leading upwards. Ascend the stairwell and greet the Watcher who stands guard over the Western Esoteric Traditions and the civilizations from which they have sprung. The Watcher observes, protects, and instructs those who would assist in its work. Be aware, however, that though it is vast and powerful, this great being requires assistants if it is to do its work fully. Passive recipients of "wisdom" and those who would leave the traditions to guard themselves do more harm through their ignorance than any enemy without. Without material contacts, the Watcher is limited.

When you are done on any of the levels, simply return the way you came and record your experiences. This practice is best done over several weeks to develop the imagery involved, and then can be done once or twice a week, intermixed with the other methods.

The Nation First

The Guardian

The Guardian[11] is by far one of the easiest rituals to perform and, amazingly, most uplifting in many respects. It seems to bring a certain "patriotic" joy that is not chauvinistic nor overly nationalistic. It is simply a deep and profound gratitude and happiness for the benefits and privileges we experience and the desire to preserve them for future generations.

Dress your altar in red. Provide for all things martial, relating to Mars or the sphere of Geburah. A pentagon in emerald green with a pentagram inscribed inside of it on red paper will be fine. Place five red candles at the pentagram's points. Be sure the uppermost point is facing upward, and that as you look upon it, the two points lowermost are towards you. Dragon's Blood or similar incense will add to the environment. If no sword is available, a clean new knife or dagger that has never been used will be fine. Simply visualize it as a larger sword for the purpose of this ritual.

Candles and incense, if used, should be lit and on the altar at this time. If known, perform the Lesser Banishing Ritual of the Pentagram. If this ritual is not known, stand erect and turn clockwise (towards your right), imaging a brilliant circle of bluish-white flame surrounding you about six feet out from where you are standing. Complete the circle and the flame as you return to face your original position.

---

[11] This ritual has been adapted from Dolores Ashcroft-Nowicki, *First Steps in Ritual: Safe, Effective Techniques for Experiencing the Inner Worlds* (Wellingborough, Northamptonshire: Aquarian Press, 1982).

Banishing should be done with your sword. If a knife or dagger is being used, imagine that it is a sword, and flaming brilliantly. Your altar should be in front of you and inside the circle as you do this.

When the circle is complete, hold the sword at the ready position, resting on your right shoulder, point up. Pause, breathe deep, and proceed.

Facing East (your original position), extend the sword forward at an angle, saluting, and say:

> Hail to you Raphael, Archangel and Guardian of the Realms of Air! Protect this our land from all approaches and guard us against follies of the mind. I am here, Raphael, to take my Watch on the Borders of the Republic. Be with me Raphael, and defend us with the Element of Air.

Turn and face the South (your right), extend the sword forward at an angle, saluting, and say:

> Hail to you Michael, Archangel and Guardian of the Realms of Fire! Protect this our land from all approaches and guard us against sudden anger or rage. I am here, Michael, to take my Watch on the Borders of the Republic. Be with me Michael, and defend us with the Element of Fire.

Turn to the West (your rear), extend the sword forward at an angle, saluting, and say:

> Hail to you Gabriel, Archangel and Guardian of the Realms of Water! Protect this our land and

guard us against sorrow and despondency in our task. I am here, Gabriel, to take my Watch on the Borders of the Republic. Be with me Gabriel, and defend us with the Element of Water.

Turn to the North (your left), extend the sword forward at an angle, saluting, and say:

Hail to you Auriel, Archangel and Guardian of the realms of Earth! Protect this our land and guard us against complacency in our task. I am here, Auriel, to take my Watch on the Borders of the Republic. Be with me Auriel, and defend us with the Element of Earth.

Turn once more, until you are facing forward again. Holding the sword at the ready position, say:

Hail to thee, Archangels of the World! Protect and Guard this our land that it may be a perfect reflection of the Heavenly realm. Remind us of our ancestors and guardians of generations past, that we may stand with them in this our time of trial. Remind us of our forefathers' pledge that this land and its people would be as a "City on the Hill" for other nations to see and emulate. Let us hold tight to this our sacred promise, vow, and obligation; and should the hosts of evil surround us, and darkness fall across the world, let the downtrodden know that we will not fail them.

Send us your Light, Strength, Power, and Wisdom. Guide our leaders in all realms of life. Purge us of those ideas that would weaken us, and forever show us the true meaning of "The New Atlantis"!

Meditate on these images, sending thoughts of peace, strength, and receptivity to divine inspiration to elected officials in all areas of government.

Arise, face the East, salute with the sword, and say:

Farewell, and peace be between us Raphael! Forever inspire us with your Wisdom!

Turn to the South, salute with the sword, and say:

Farewell, and peace be between us Michael! Forever instill us with your Courage!

Turn and face the West, salute with the sword, and say:

Farewell, and peace be between us Gabriel! Forever support us with your Compassion!

Turn and face the North, salute with the sword, and say:

Farewell, and peace be between us Auriel! Forever increase our Patience and Strength!

Turn until you are facing the East once again.

Pause. Extinguish the candles on the altar. Take your sword and, turning counter-clockwise, imagine that the circle is being erased, and that everything is returned to normal.

Ring a bell, stomp your foot, or clap your hands five times to reinforce this notion. The ritual is ended.

This ritual can be substantially increased and modified by an experienced ritualist. Archetypal imagery, as well as symbols such as the Great Seal of the United States or its reverse side with the "Eye in the Triangle" imagery, can be added to strengthen national symbols in the collective psyche. A folded American flag in the shape of a triangle with the star field uppermost on the altar in the center of the green pentagon/pentagram image would be a valuable addition. The Great Seal could also be placed there for strengthening its power as a talismanic image. Individuals from history can be placed at the quarters and called up along with, or in place of, the archangels.

King, Hierophant, and Warrior in a Democracy

Traditional archetypes of leadership do not easily translate over into a democratic model. However, there are some personalities that we can elevate to "archetype" status because of distance and the historical idealizing of their roles. The most important models are those which connect us to divinely inspired leadership in our government through the influences of Chesed/Jupiter, divinely inspired action in our military (as it follows civilian direction) via the influences of Geburah/Mars, and divinely inspired spiritual leadership through our traditional spiritual institutions, through the influences of Tiphareth/Sun and Yesod/Moon.

To do this, we suggest that each person or group working these rituals build up over a period of time an archetypal image based on historical personages and the above-associated symbolism to influence these areas of our collective life. For example, one might use George Washington or Roosevelt as an archetype of powerful leadership in war and crises and General Patton or General Pershing for creative, aggressive, and successful military command. Spiritual leadership is tricky, as the United States has never had an official religion or church. However, several figures have had a prominent, if understated, effect on American history. Conrad Beissel of the Ephrata community; Johannes Kelpius, the Hermit (sometimes called "Wizard") of the Wissahickon; Albert Pike, Grand Commander of the Ancient and Accepted Scottish Rite of Freemasonry; and the mysterious "Envoi" mentioned frequently by Manly P. Hall[12] are just a few that fulfill the role of a Merlin or court wizard, while being beyond sect or politics. A generic figure—decked in eighteenth-century Masonic regalia—would also do just fine for this work. This figure is concerned mostly with right ethics, morals, and decisions that affect the character of the nation and its forward progress.

When the archetype has been developed, it should be projected on to or seen as influencing its sphere of activity through a symbol for the area of government or society that it affects. For example, the symbols used could be simply the Pentagon for the military; a combined image of the White House and Congress for the government and leadership; and a generic "house of worship" or the media

---

[12]See: Manly P. Hall, *The Secret Destiny of America* (New York: J. P. Tarcher/Penguin, 2008) and Robert Hieronimus, *America's Secret Destiny: A Spiritual Vision and the Founding of a Nation* (Rochester, VT: Destiny Books, 1989).

(since attendance is down in these institutions) for spiritual progress and development.

This projection can be done alone or in connection with the Inner Sanctum, during the meditation phase. The dominant color for government and civilian life is blue with some flashing orange highlights, representing the influence of Jupiter. The dominant color for military activities is red with some flashing green highlights, representing the influence of Mars. The dominant color for spiritual activities is violet, with some shades of purple, and intense gold highlights, representing the influence of the Sun and the Moon combined (but with stronger emphasis on the Moon, or human psyche and personality).

The Ring-Pass-Not

This is the easiest of the practices presented. It consists of imagining the continental United States (or whatever country you are performing this ritual for), with Alaska and Hawaii included, surrounded by a brilliant wall of piercing red flame. This is the purifying and defending energy of Geburah/Mars. This flame is solid, like a wall of light, and patrolled by the Seraphim, the angelic host of warriors under the direction of Khamael, the archangel of Geburah. The image is built up with the intention that all negativity, evil, and acts of war or terrorism are kept *out*. For the sake of the visualization, they can be imagined as being detached and off the coast of California as on many maps. This practice can be done alone, from the Inner Sanctum, or in the Tower of Vision.

Dispersing the Clouds of War

Michael

Michael is said to have been present during the "War in the Heavens," during which he defeated the rebellious host of angels led by Lucifer, who after his "fall" was known as Satan, or the "One Who Opposes." This symbolism gives us much to work with once we have firmly established our Inner Sanctum and made contact with the additional energies present there. We can call upon them to strengthen and purify our land and culture first, and then ask that they go forth and cleanse the land of others, creating an environment beneficial to the further progress of its people.

When calling on Michael, be sure that you are firmly established in your Inner Sanctum. Then, mentally or verbally call on Michael to come and assist in the work at hand. Sense Michael's presence, and visualize him in his traditional form, as a winged angel carrying a spear or sword pointed downward, with red cape, wearing armor (often Roman). Ask that he go forth and cleanse the air around the war zone of Iraq, Palestine, or any other area you are drawn to assist, and imagine him flying off and over the area with his legions. See their great spears and swords piercing the dark clouds of war and hate. Imagine the clouds reeling back, and clearing away. Imagine that as they clear, the brilliant light and warmth of the sun reaches through, and the people and ground below feel its life-giving warmth and at peace.

Azrael's Wings: Cleansing the Temple

This work is performed in the same way as above, with Michael, except that the "Recording Angel of Life and Death" is called upon instead to do the work with his many legions. Instead of a general area—such as a country or city—a specific mosque or temple that is being used to generate hate and ill will is utilized as the recipient of the energy. Once again, from your Inner Sanctum, call upon Azrael. Feel his presence and willingness to assist in the work. Imagine him and his legions above the specific temple, entering into it from above. Imagine the angels cleansing the negative energy, scattering it with their mere presence, and see them whispering into the ears of those present to turn their hearts away from the message of death to a message of the inner life.

When you have finished with any of the above practices, mentally return to the Inner Sanctum and end your session.

Khamael and the Weapons of War

The archangel Khamael rules Geburah and directs its energies through the planet Mars. Khamael can be invoked during the "Guardian Ritual," during the meditation phase, and asked to purify, strengthen, and make manifest the highest ideals of the land, and to reign in those ideas and persons that would spread war, discord, and hate. His weapons are the sword for direct combat of ideas; the whip for pushing forward when inertia would take over; the chain for binding or "imprisoning" the opposition so that it cannot spread; the shield for defense of the innocent and weak; and the spear for the projection of force over great distances. Khamael,

Michael, and Azrael, when taken in this manner, share many of the same characteristics. Michael and Khamael are often pictured in a similar manner.

Additional Technical Considerations

Experienced ritualists may want to consider the following when working the more advanced aspects of this paper.

1. Given the close relationship between Islamic Fundamentalism, terrorism, and the physical places of worship, it would be advantageous to focus the act of dispersal at the "dark clouds of war and evil" that are concentrated over the mosques used by specific clerics and leaders.

2. Islam is closely allied with the crescent and color green; as such the planetary days and hours of Luna and Venus would be advantageous times for this work.

3. The Archangel Gabriel delivered the Koran to Mohammed; as such invoking and assuming the Godform of Gabriel during this phase of the work would be advantageous.

Conclusion

Esotericists do not live in a vacuum. Despite many who would like to exist in their own world of ideas, the world of action comes knocking at our door, and in times of crisis, crashes right through. If esotericism is to demonstrate that it is practical, meaningful, and relevant to our modern life, it must take up the standard and fight for what is right on its plane of expertise, the domain of the mind. Be clear on this point: the current war is very much an "Aquarian" war in which weapons of the air will figure prominently, as will the "air waves" of mass communication, hidden and encrypted communications, electronics, disinformation, and above all the regions of the human mind. If esotericists do not take their place in the ranks they, along with all that they stand for, will be swept away into the dustbin of history. This is a battle for the world soul—to stand on the sidelines is to fight for evil.

Summary

1. The current crisis in human development threatens the very existence of civilization, and therefore requires that practical esotericists actively seek to promote and nurture healthy, peaceful, and progressive conditions within their own governments and in the Middle East in particular.

2. Occult methods have historically been employed by esoteric orders and organizations during times of national and international crises.

3. The collective mind is easily led, even distracted. This allows the collective unconscious to be manipulated by a variety of factors: political, religious, and commercial.

4. Evil exists in three forms: error or sin, excess, and conscious decisions to do harm. It is the latter that is called "positive evil," and it is *true* evil in the mystical sense. Error and excess are part of the human learning process.

5. It is critical that we stay *apolitical* in this work, and focus on the broad goal and not the specific means by which the outcome should manifest.

6. Generating good will and impersonal compassion are the main emotional tools of this work.

7. Negative constructs require constant new sources of fresh emotional energy to exist, as they have limited momentum and collapse in on themselves without it.

8. Disconnecting a negative and destructive leadership from its supply of emotional energy is done on the subconscious level, and can be done using prayer, ritual, and meditation, as they work telepathically on the individuals being used.

9. A leadership without a membership base or source of emotional energy becomes limited in its ability to project power, and will be replaced.

10. Humanity is constantly seeking to align its visions of justice with the cosmic ideal of justice.

11. The ancient Egyptian concept of Maat, or Universal Order and Justice, is mirrored in the qabalistic idea of Daäth.

12. Daäth is an ideal of the Cosmic Mind free of human notions, and is very abstract. It is also closely allied with the subconscious, or Yesod, so that those ideas can enter into human activity.

Support from the Institute for Hermetic Studies

The Institute for Hermetic Studies offers a range of ongoing support to individual students and groups through online materials, seminars, and private tutorial. These include but are not limited to: basic, intermediate, and advanced instruction in the Hermetic Arts and Sciences, astrological consultations, assistance with psychic and spiritual crises, and training for ordination in the Minor and Major Orders of the Church of St. Cyprian the Mage of Antioch. All information regarding our programs is announced in our free electronic newsletter VOXHERMES. For more information contact:

> The Institute for Hermetic Studies
> P.O. Box 4513
> Wyoming, PA 18644-04513
>
> www.hermeticinstitute.org
> info@hermeticinstitute.org

Mark Stavish (Pennsylvania) is a respected authority in the study and practice of Western spiritual traditions. He is the author of several books, most recently the IHS Monograph Series and the preceding volumes of IHS Study Guides, *Light on the Path*, *The Inner Way*, *Child of the Sun*, and *Words of My Teachers*, as well as *The Path of Alchemy*, *Kabbalah for Health and Wellness*, and *Between the Gates: Lucid Dreaming, Astral Projection, and the Body of Light in Western Esotericism*. His works have been translated into nine languages worldwide. He is founder of both the Institute for Hermetic Studies (Wyoming, Pennsylvania), where he is Director of Studies, and the Louis Claude de St. Martin Fund, a non-profit fund dedicated to the study and practice of esotericism.

Alfred DeStefano III (Virginia) is a college mathematics instructor. He is editor of the IHS Monograph Series and has assisted in the production of numerous esoteric publications, including the previous volumes of IHS Study Guides and the 7th Edition of Israel Regardie's *The Golden Dawn*, edited by John Michael Greer (Llewellyn).

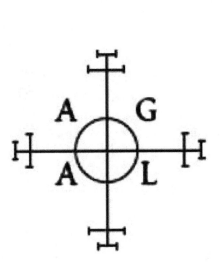

CPSIA information can be obtained
at www.ICGtesting.com
Printed in the USA
LVHW012206050519
616736LV00029B/859